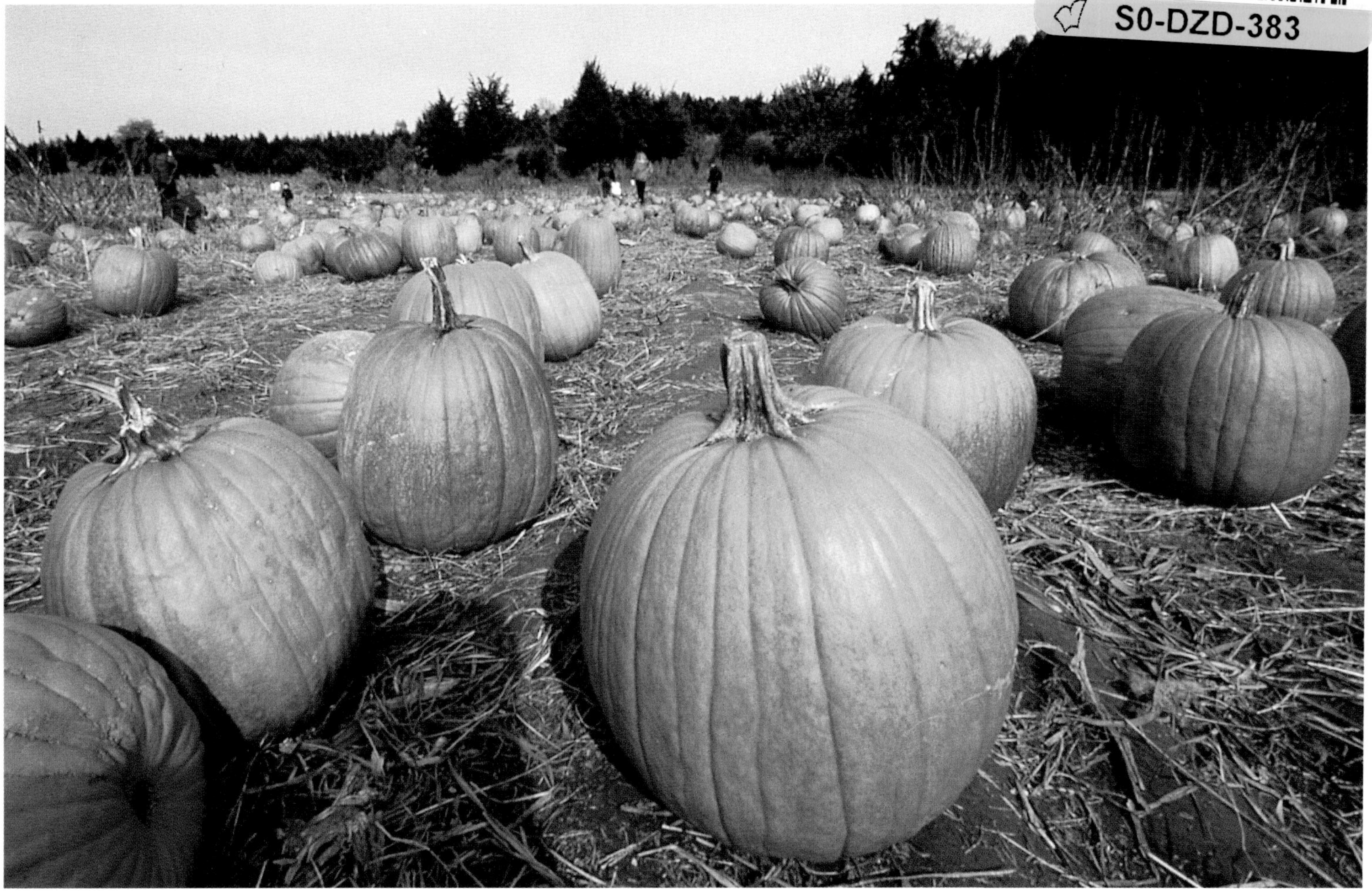

pumpkins

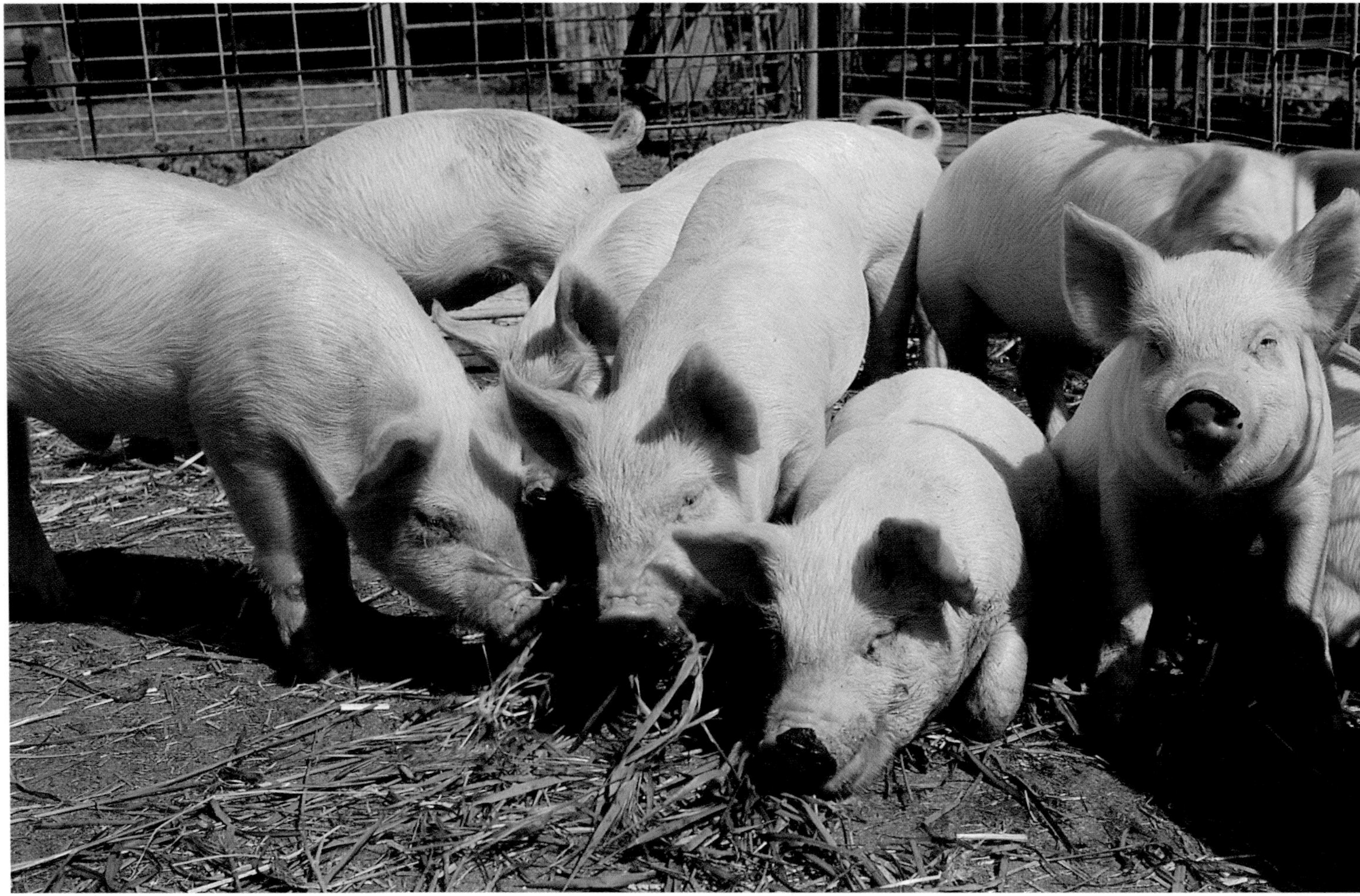

pigs

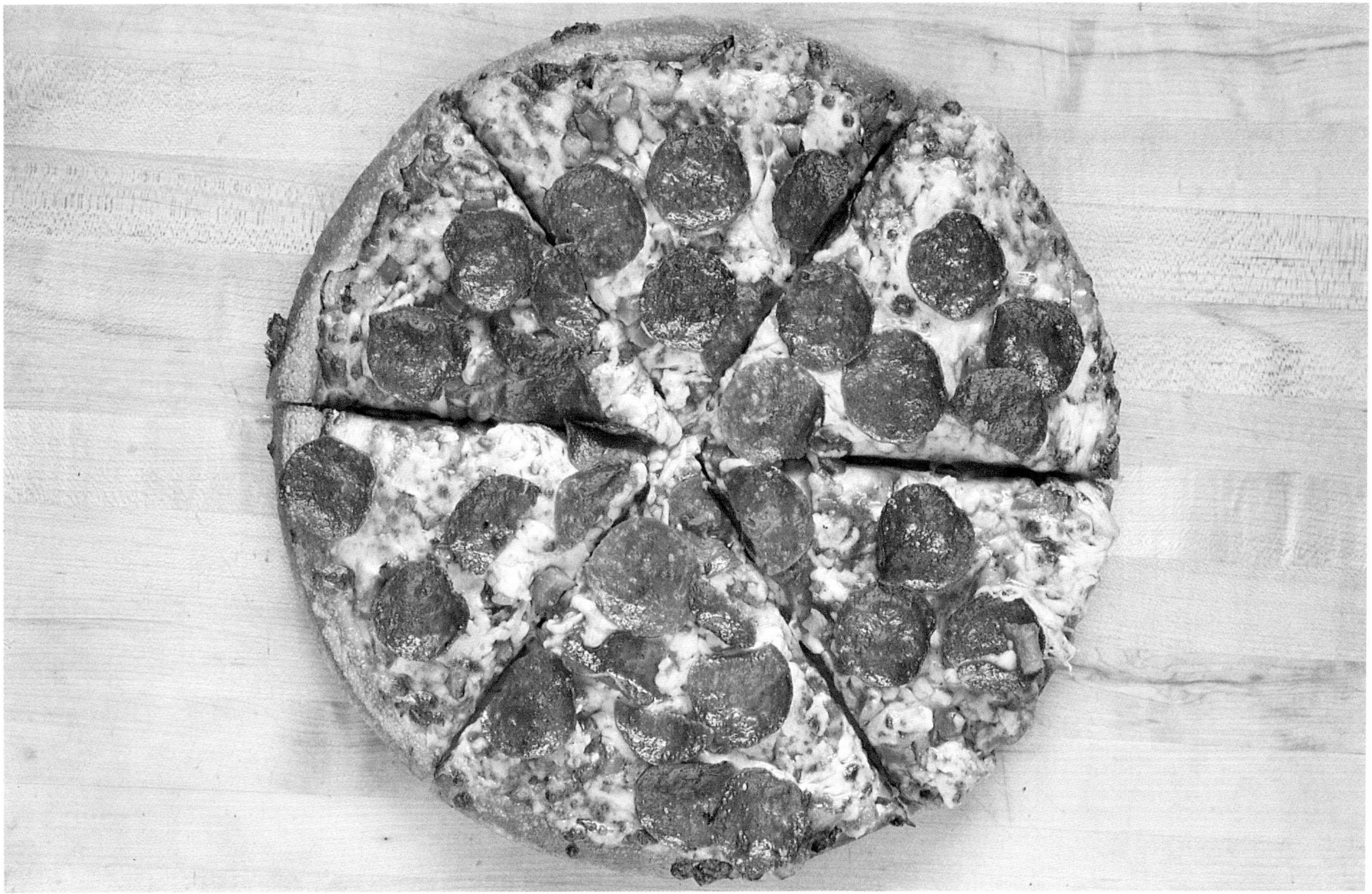

pizza

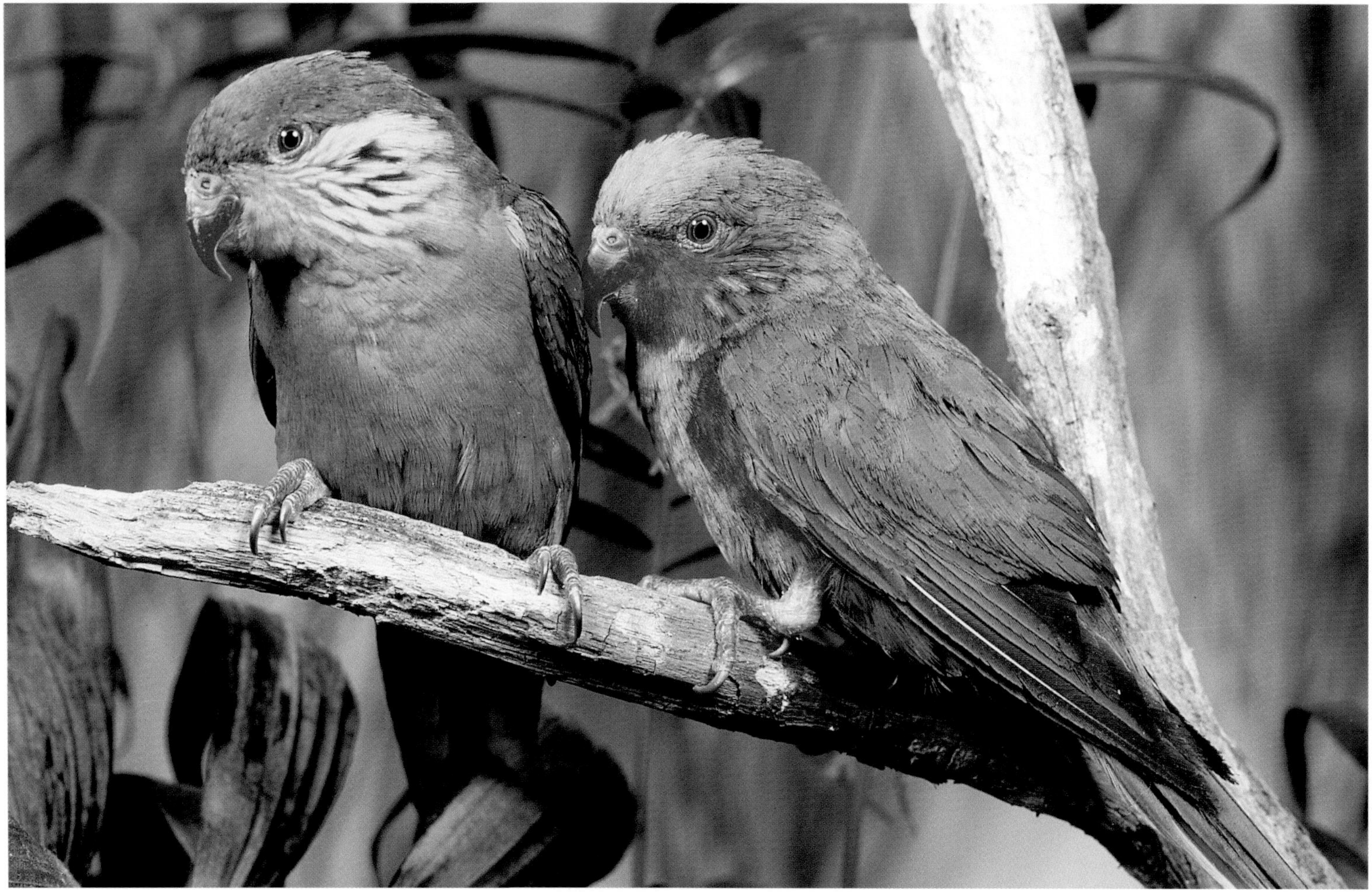

parrots

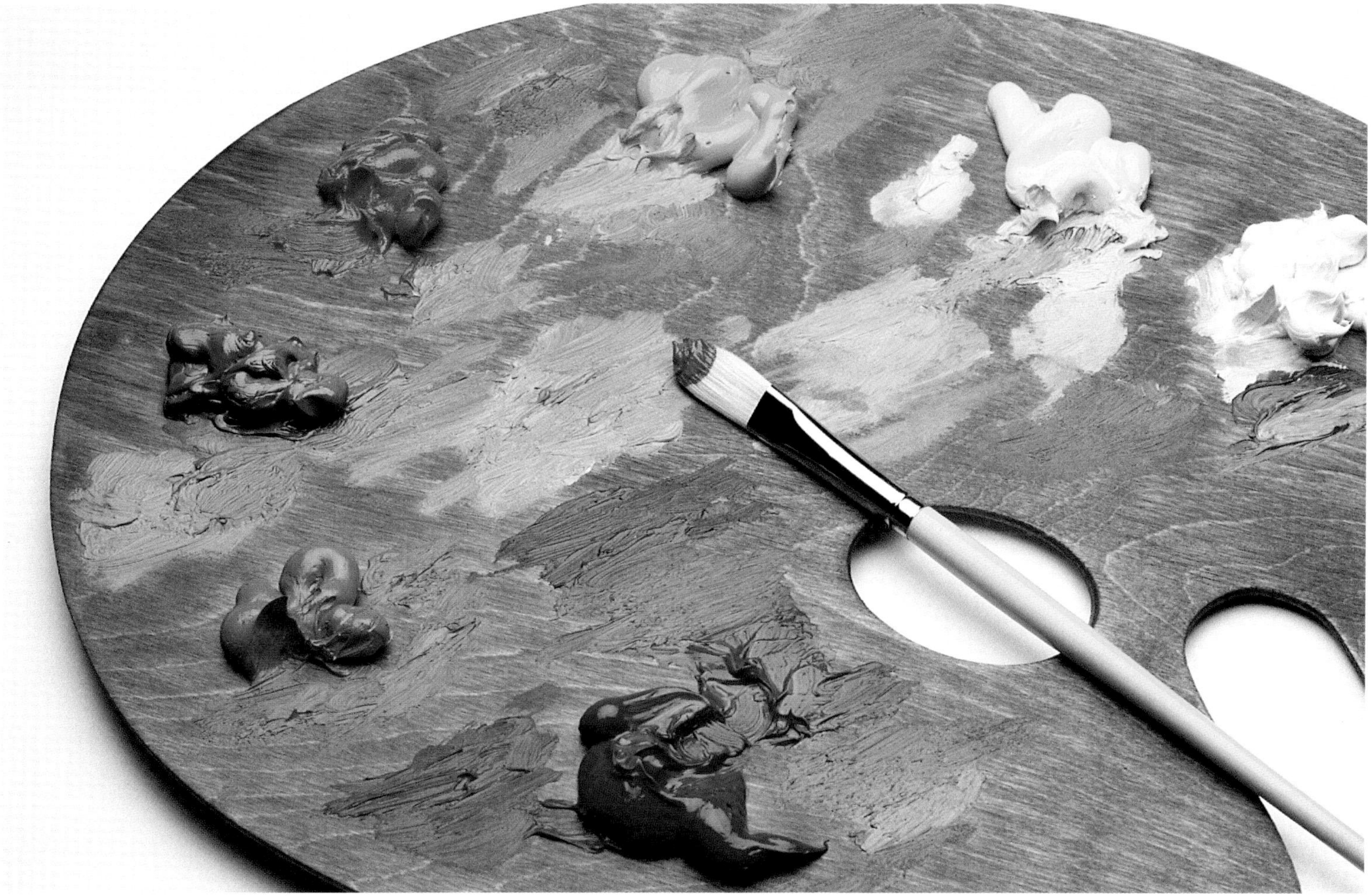

paints

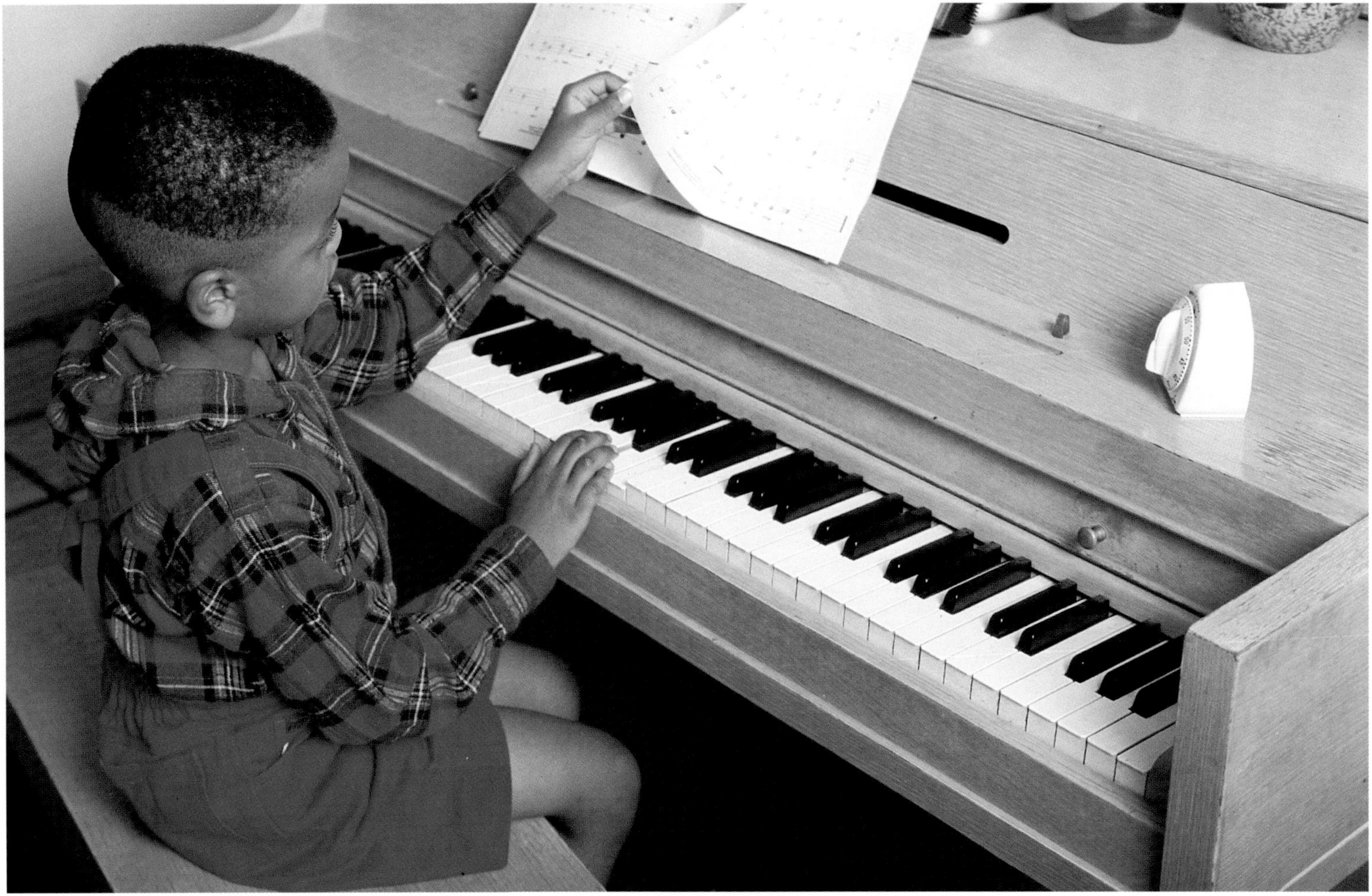

piano

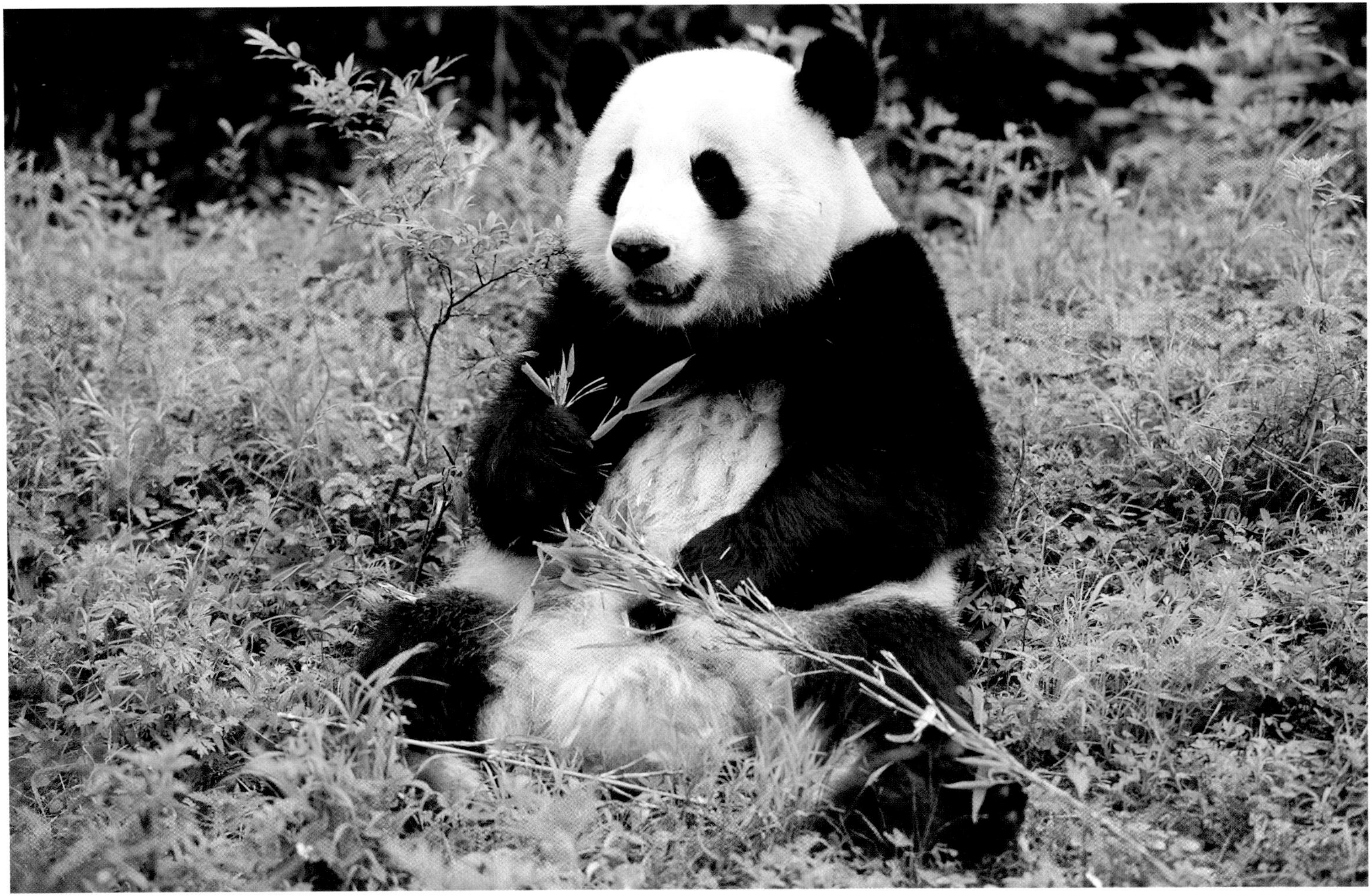

panda

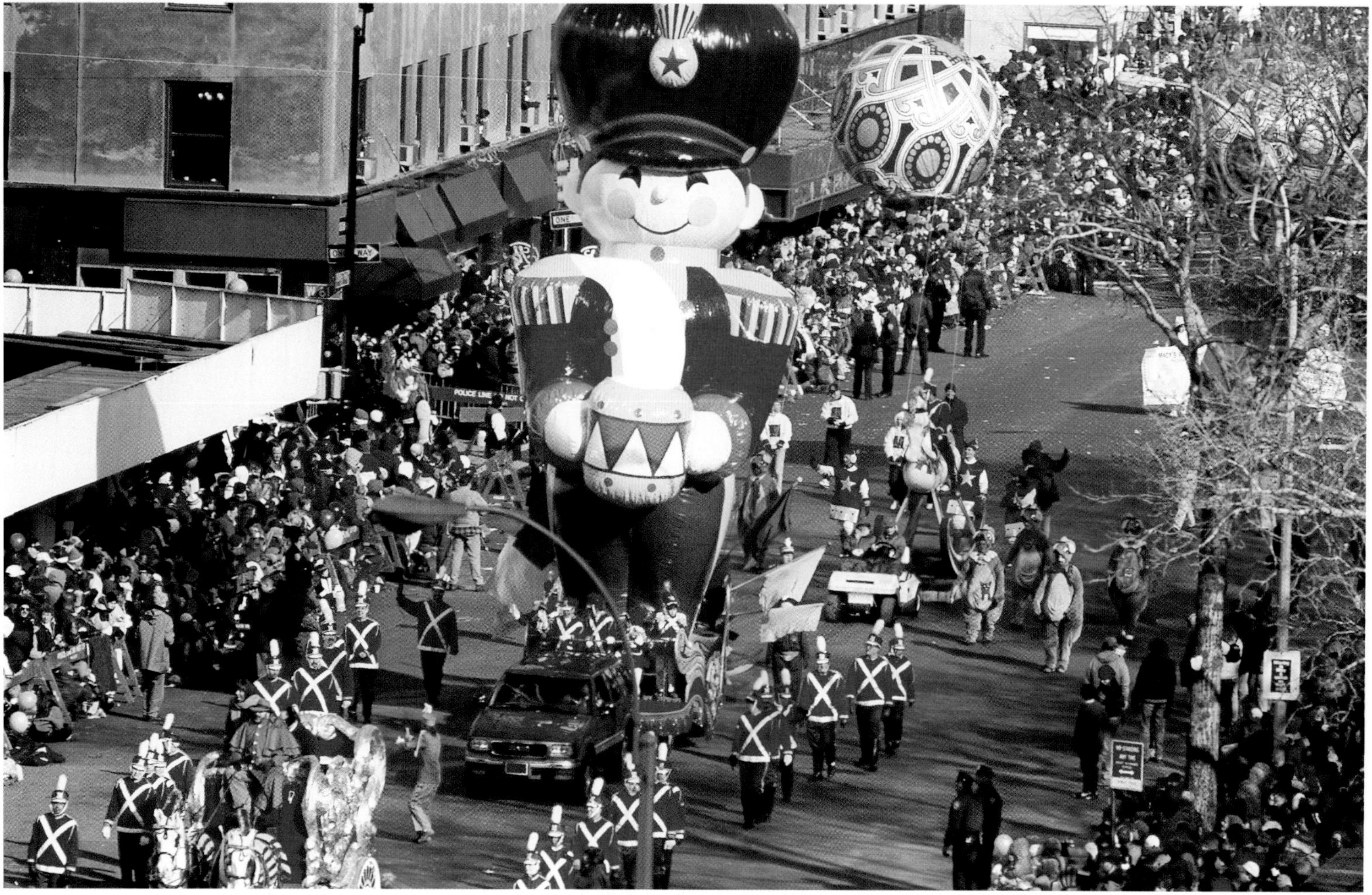

parade